grad... on ...
Dig the ride!
Rick Dale

The Beat Handbook

100 Days of Kerouactions

Rick Dale

ISBN: 1-4392-0474-8
ISBN-13: 9781439204740

Visit www.booksurge.com to order additional copies.

DEDICATION

This book is dedicated to my hero, Jack; my inspiration, Keith; my life partner and editor, Crystal; my son, Jason; my mom, Elizabeth; my writing guru, Kath; and, my beat poet friend, Charlie.

TABLE OF CONTENTS

INTRODUCTION

Jack Kerouac was a man of action.[1] When in doubt, he *did* something. Not always something we might consider healthy – drinking, engaging in promiscuous sex, and abusing drugs – or legal –
stealing food, gasoline, and clothing – but at least he *acted*.[2] This
is not to ignore the fact that he was an intellectual, too, with a
complex, inquisitive, and rich inner life.

In fact, it was Kerouac's deep intellectualism that drove him to
action. "The greatest problem for him to resolve, he stated, was to find
an 'art-method' capable of unleashing the inner life" (Nicosia, 1994,
p. 148).[3][4] About his excesses, he would say that they were all in the
name of gathering experience about which to write. "Whatever

---

1   I am not going to attempt even a brief biography of Jack
Kerouac. That has been done and done well. See Gerald Nicosia's
Memory Babe: A Critical Biography of Jack Kerouac if you want to know
about Jack's life and times.
2   Here is the one-time legal caveat you'll find in this book: the
author is not responsible for any action you, the reader, takes as a result
of advice contained herein. All advice is to be evaluated by the reader
for its potential consequences, and any and all outcomes of such
actions – positive or negative – are the sole responsibility of the reader.
In other words, if you act stupid and get in trouble, or worse, the author
is not liable. It's a book, for heaven's sakes. Use your brain, not mine.
(Tangential note: A high school student of mine used to ask me questions he could easily look up, and when I asked him why he did that, he
always replied, "Why use my brain when I can use yours?")
3   This and all subsequent quotes in this book – being duly-cited,
small excerpts used in a work of criticism/commentary/scholarship and
having no impact on the potential market for or value of the copyright-
ed works – fall under the Fair Use guidelines of copyright law under 17
USC Section 107.
4   If you are not familiar with American Psychological Association
(APA) style, which I have used to cite references in this book, here's a
quick lesson. When you see author names or dates or page numbers
within parentheses within the text, it is letting you know which of the
entries under References at the end of the book is the source of that
particular quote or idea.

they [he and Allen Ginsburg] did in the present didn't matter as long as they emerged from it wiser and more capable.... Jack continuously talked about how he would use his drug experience as a writer" (p. 148). This sentiment held true for Kerouac regarding all his activities, and his love affair with America acknowledged its paradoxes by not trying to solve them (p. 155). "The liberal-radical quest to 'find the answers' would get one irretrievably lost. Jack's way, like that of pioneer America, was *to live the answers*" (p. 155).

Given the title of this book – *The Beat Handbook* – I thought perhaps a brief explanation for non-Kerouac fans is in order. Kerouac is credited with inventing the term "beat" and the phrase "beat generation" to describe the generation just before the hippie generation of the sixties. Some say feminist writer Gertrude Stein coined the phrase and Kerouac borrowed it from her. No matter, because Kerouac is routinely credited with the term. He is therefore "considered to be the father of the beat movement, therefore the grandfather of the hippie movement. [He was] definitely the predominant author of beat literature" (McCleary, 2002, p. 272).

My premise: "beatness" is the condition of living as a "beat," and it's a desirable way to live, especially in today's materialistic, fast-paced culture. A good way to discern what "beatness" looks like is to take our cues directly from the father of the beat generation, Jack Kerouac. I have decided to do that by mining his writings, particularly his quasi-autobiographical fiction, but also his journals and letters.[5] Future sequels may delve into Kerouac's other books, journals, and letters. I mined for two things: suggested behaviors and actual behaviors. That is, if Kerouac offered advice, or if Kerouac (or a beat character) did it, I figure that makes it a beat behavior. I could be wrong about that. And I don't care.

---

5   Note: This book only mined The Dharma Bums (Kerouac, 1976) and On The Road (Kerouac, 1976).

I *do* care that you do not mistake the tenor of this book as sexist. I hope you can keep in mind that Kerouac likely would be considered highly racist, sexist, and misogynistic in today's culture. I am not going to disguise that, given that I am taking my lead from what he wrote, regardless of whether it is politically correct.

Why 100 days? Honestly, the original subtitle was *365 Days of Kerouactions* (there being 365 days in a year and this being a book that one might use as a daily reader). Closing in on 100 entries, I realized that – serendipitously – I was going to produce about 100 entries[6] out of *The Dharma Bums* and *On The Road*. Not wanting to force entries to reach a somewhat arbitrary number, I decided to leave room for sequels to this book, using *Big Sur*, *Desolation Angels*, and other Kerouac books. Why not do the latter right up front? Too much work and I wanted to get something in print[7].

How to Use This Book

Words! Kerouac used plenty of them but ultimately they are only signposts to something else. Much better to scale Everest than to read about it, but better to read about it than never experience it at all. So what would Kerouac do regarding this book? Stop wasting time reading it, for one thing! Grab your backpack – or buy (from a Goodwill store, not new for heaven's sakes) or borrow one or, better, find one in a dumpster – throw some Rye-Krisps, salami, cheese, and water in there and head out. Throw this book in there, too, so you can use it as a journal. Or just throw it away. If you do the latter, make sure you litter a public highway cutting through a pristine wilderness area because the highway shouldn't be there in the first place and you'd at least make eco-terrorist Edward Abbey happy and probably Kerouac, too, although Abbey

---

6   For a while I shot for 101, but serendipitously ended up with exactly 100. I petered out and the book ended.
7   Brad Blanton (1996) might call this statement "radical honesty."

didn't think Kerouac ended up too well (and neither do I), saying, "Jack Kerouac, like a sick refrigerator, worked too hard at keeping cool and died on his mama's lap from alcohol and infantilism."[8]

Now I don't agree with Abbey's sentiment although his facts may be correct and you may be wondering why I inserted an Abbey reference (and a negative one at that) here and some of you unbearable unconscious academics will be fussing about the appropriateness of it or the accuracy of the quote and the fact of the matter is I did it because this is *my* book – not yours – and I have no literacy standards to which I must adhere and further-more I wrote this book because I love Jack Kerouac (no, not in *that* way) and because I wanted to have fun and I love Edward Abbey, too, so why can't I insert references to whatever and whomever I want? Well, I can. And I did. And if you don't like it, remember that I told you several sentences ago that you were wasting your time reading this when you could be out "on the road" experiencing life. One of the things about this day and age that would infuriate Kerouac would have to be the proliferation of rules about what you can and cannot do, not the least of which is The Patriot Act but one need look no further than a pack of cigarettes to see how government is intruding on our every activity and at least Kerouac and Abbey lived true to their own callings and didn't bow down to every culturally and politically correct rule and standard and expectation. No doubt the biggest danger facing this generation is compliance, or as George Bernanos so eloquently put it.

> It will not be cruelty that will be responsible for our extinction and still less, of course, the indignation that cruelty awakens and the reprisals and vengeance that it brings upon itself . . . but the docility, the lack of responsibility of the modern

---

8   From http://www.abbeyweb.net/quotes.htx?query=Kerouac&o p=search.

man, his base subservient acceptance of every common decree. The horrors that we have seen, the still greater horrors we shall presently see, are not signs that rebels, insubordinate, untamable men are increasing in number throughout the world, but rather that there is a constant increase in the number of obedient, docile men (as cited in Rosenberg, 2005, pp. 21-22).

Hell, the beat generation was all about revolting against mainstream America, and so in that spirit I will revolt against anyone and everything whenever I can and that includes writing this book![9]

My Purpose In Writing This Book

So why did I write this book? As alluded to earlier, I love Kerouac and I wanted to have fun. And of course I want you to have fun reading it. But what else did I have in mind? Certainly, I wanted to bring Kerouac to a new generation, not in a scholarly way – as I am not a Kerouac scholar – but in a way that would make Kerouac accessible in a format similar to the successful *What Would Such-and-Such Do?* series. That is, I wanted to combine accessing Kerouac with some advice on how to live.

I feel duty-bound to state at the outset that this entire effort is somewhat "tongue-in-cheek," and I would be the first to admit that using Kerouac as a role model for our actions would be somewhat questionable. Or would it? At least he lived while he lived.[10]

---

9   As I am re-reading this passage right after writing Day 82 (on August 22, 2006), I am reading George Carlin's *When Will Jesus Bring the Porkchops?* George is a funny guy, but he is also brilliant, insightful, noncompliant, and beat! (And, as of June 22, 2008, dead.)
10   As Jonathan Swift said, "May you live all the days of your life."

And given Kerouac's Buddhist perspective and practice (there is, after all, a popular book titled, *What Would Buddha Do?*), I have to think that he would smile to see such an effort. I have found, in the course of this writing effort – which I affectionately code-named "The Project" – that asking yourself, or another person, "What would Kerouac do?" actually serves a useful – if not humorous – purpose by forcing someone at an indecisive moment to "get off the dime" so to speak and think about a problem from a different perspective.[11] Often my answer to this question has been obvious but unhelpful in the practical world – for example, the answer might be to go get drunk – but even that answer would cause a smile or a chuckle and at least elevate my mood.

So expect some serious deliberation as well as some lightheartedness as you make your way through what follows. When faced with one of life's little or big challenges, ask yourself, "What would Kerouac do?" Why, he would act of course. I have discerned the answers to this important question from his own admittedly autobiographical fiction writings, not from the ramblings of scholars.

You don't have to "live the answer," as he likely would. You can just smile. Or you can act. Either way, it's all good.

It is my fervent hope that you use this book as you see fit! That is, as a daily calendar reading – if that meets your needs – or as a reference – looking up readings by topic (see the Table of Contents) – or as a journal (lots of white space has been provided: real beats are writers!) – or as a straight-through read. Or something to prop up a broken table. As you wish!

---

11   An original title for this book was *What Would Kerouac Do?*

"Kerouactions"

I have dubbed the answer to "What would Kerouac do?" a "Kerouaction." I think that's fairly clever, and while I would love to see the term in Webster's some day, I know better than that and will take my satisfaction from the fact that I came up with it at all. It would be payback enough if one other human being on the planet ever used the term,[12] even if only to criticize me for inventing it. I hope I don't take criticism to heart quite like Jack did, and I would dearly love to find out if fame could drive me madder than I already am. Each reading also includes a suggested "Kerouactivity." That's for readers who need someone to tell them what to do. It's okay. We all look for that in one form or another (religion, government, experts, leaders, *authors*). If you don't like a suggested Kerouactivity, make up your own but remember to *go go go*.

In its original form, this book presented a quoted passage from either *The Dharma Bums* (1976) or *On The Road* (1976), followed by my comments on the passage. I approached a New York agent (is that like a "Philadelphia lawyer"?) who ran screaming for the hills about how the Kerouac estate would never ever give permission for such a work.

So, I said "Fuck it, Dude! Let's go bowling,"[13] and edited out all those wonderful passages. I left the entries in order, starting at the beginning of *Bums* and ending at the end of *Road*. That means, with a little effort and ingenuity, you could identify every passage that triggered an entry.[14] Look at it as a treasure hunt. It would

---

12   I mean use in a serious way in an authentic context. My sales rep from BookSurge, Kelly, told me on the phone that it was her new favorite word, but that doesn't really count. No offense, Kelly.
13   A movie reference, which is a beat thing to do. See Day 48.
14   If you identify every entry by page number, let me know on my website: www.thebeathandbook.com.

help if you had the same editions I used (see References). Since I purposely left entries in the order they occurred, you'll note some repetition of topics that might otherwise be combined.

Anyway, what you have in your hands is my good faith compromise to keep the copyright police away from my door. I'm pretty sure I can talk *about* Jack's books. I imagine the word Kerouaction could get me in trouble. I hope so. That would generate mad publicity and I might actually find a traditional publisher.

I invite you to enjoy what follows, and sincerely hope that Jack, his family, and fans around the world will see this book for what I intend: a monument to my hero, Jack Kerouac, the beatest guy who ever lived.

DAY 1

Today's Kerouaction: On Vegetarianism

In this age of diet fads, a particular passage in *The Dharma* Bums (Kerouac, 1976) is especially relevant. My friend, Keith – to whom this book is in part dedicated – is a fairly dyed-in-the-wool (I wonder where that term comes from?) vegetarian and yet he introduced me to Kerouac so we have some interesting conversations about whether vegetarianism is beat or not or maybe it doesn't matter much at all in the grand scheme of things.

The Kerouaction suggested here is simple: eat what you want. You have my permission. For other specific suggestions on what to eat, see Days 17, 19, 24, 52, 54, and 57.[15]

Suggested Kerouactivity:

Listen to your body and write down what you are hungry for right now without regard to whether it is "healthy."

---

15   I wrote this – my first entry – around January 2005. Now I see on television in December 2005 – 12 months later – a new diet fad called the No Diet Diet. The advice: eat what you want, just not so much of it. I heard the author in an interview call it "intuitive eating." This is simply evidence that everything you need to know is already known and has been known for a long time. All you have to do is discover it. Most of the time, it lies within you. Intuitive eating! Kerouac advised us on this "new" concept 50 years ago! And, as I write this sentence on January 8, 2008, I realize from some reading I did today that Jiddu Krishnamurti advised the same approach in *Beyond Violence* (1973).

DAY 2

Today's Kerouaction:
On Sex as Meditation

Japhy and Princess engage in sexual intercourse in front of Smith (Kerouac). However, it is not for the purpose of sexual gratification, but as a form of meditation. According to the Encyclopedia Brittanica Online, "yabyum" – in Buddhist art of India, Nepal, and Tibet – is the representation of the male deity in sexual embrace with his female consort. The pose is generally understood to represent the mystical union of the active force, or method (*upaya,* conceived of as masculine), with wisdom *(prajna,* conceived of as feminine) – a fusion necessary to overcome the false duality.

So the point here is that we Westerners have a narrow view of intercourse – how it is to be done and why – and I suggest you find someone to try yabyum with (yes, I know I ended that sentence with a preposition – my beat poet friend Charlie says to do that fearlessly). But not your current lover! She or he would probably want it to be about sex (or love-making)! Maybe it would be best to find someone to whom you are not attracted in order to practice this particular activity?

Suggested Kerouactivity:

Ask your yoga teacher if s/he knows what yabyum is. You'll know what to do next depending on his/her answer.

DAY 3

Today's Kerouaction: On College

Don't go to college. It's a waste of time and money. Lots of smart, successful people didn't. Suggested Kerouaction: go to your local library and start reading the first book on the left hand side of the top shelf in the northeast corner of the first floor. Work your way through every book in the library, sequentially from where you started. When you are done – if that is even possible – start on the new books that have arrived since you started. In the meantime, enjoy what becoming educated feels like. Remember that J. Krishnamurti distinguished between knowledge and wisdom and Carl Rogers said that significant learning did not occur unless your behavior or attitude or even your personality changed.

But if you're at a college – either as a professor or a student – be original and don't fall prey to institutional and societal norms and values. Follow your own path! Heed the advice of Henry David Thoreau and be a nonconformist. Kerouac admired Thoreau, and so pretty much anything Thoreau advised is a Kerouaction in waiting!

"Grooming schools for the middle-class non-identity" (Kerouac, 1976b, p. 39)? Ouch! That is some indictment, and I'm not seeing that things are much better. If anything, they are worse, given the corporatization of the university and the resulting disintegration of what limited amounts of academic freedom there were in the first place (for example, see Jennifer Washburn's 2005 book, *University, Inc.: The Corporate Corruption of Higher Education*).

Suggested Kerouactivity:

Write down 10 people who have most influenced you over your lifetime. Put a checkmark next to those who went to college. There is no right or wrong answer here – it's just information for you to do with what you wish. You might also consider letting those 10 people know what they meant to you. Too often we neglect that important action until it's too late.

DAY 4

Today's Kerouaction: On Crap

Simple. Go take a shit in the woods once in a while. It's good for you. Gets you back to nature. There is a whole book on the subject in case you don't have a clue how to do it (Meyer, 1994). And stop washing your hands so much, especially with antibacterial soap. As comedian George Carlin said, your immune system needs practice to stay healthy and functioning. Give it some germs once in a while! Finally, while this is not so much an action as a piece of advice, quit taking yourself so damn seriously. Think about where we are all going to end up: dead and rotting or burned away. Or something.

Suggested Kerouactivity:

Describe the last time you took a shit outside without the benefit of some man-made contraption. If you never have or it's been so long you can't remember, go outside right now and create something to write about! I could tell you a story about my way home from work one night, but I won't . . . . TMI.[16]

---

16   I'm not sure what Jack would think about such acronyms, especially those that have evolved because of text messaging and live chat (ROFL, BRB, JK, etc.). The important thing is, what do you think he would think?

DAY 5

Today's Kerouaction:
On Fresh Air, the Dharma, and Drinking

Many Kerouactions here! First, get the Hell outside and enjoy the fresh air. Smith (Kerouac) references The Place at the beginning of his climb up Matterhorn with Japhy. The Place is a watering hole where they could be drunk and bleary and sick instead of outside in the pristine fresh air about to climb a mountain. Second, study some Buddhism and figure out the dharma for yourself!

Highly recommended books on this topic include anything by Alan Watts or Thich Nhat Hanh or Pema Chodron or Charlotte Joko Beck or Sylvia Boorstein. Third – and this is a tough one to discern – do what you can to moderate your drinking. In this particular instance, Kerouac is saying what he ought to do and not what he did. In fact, he drank himself to death (so some say). So I guess I'm going to take the hypocritical (?) path and tell you to do what he said (and tried to do but failed), not what he actually did.

A friend of mine is drinking himself to death as I write this. Sad but true.

Suggested Kerouactivity:

My friend, Keith, says Kerouac's drink of choice was Jack Daniels and ginger ale. I haven't bothered to confirm that, but I do know that it's tasty. You can figure out the suggested Kerouactivity here without me spelling it out for you.

Cheers.

DAY 6

Today's Kerouaction: On Materialism

I already told you in the introduction to throw this book away and grab your backpack and get going! Add to that praying on a mountain and you're most of the way there. Except one more thing: rent *Fight Club* and watch it – carefully. And remember, you are not your car. You are not your job. You are not your bald head. Or your failing member (that was for my 50+ year-old friends). Yair![17]

Suggested Kerouactivity:

Write a poem in this space. A haiku will do (3 lines: 5 syllables, 7 syllables, 5 syllables – or, ignore that sophomoric rule shit and follow your own haiku structure).

---

17   "Yair" is beat for an emphatic "yes."

DAY 7

Today's Kerouaction:
On Finding a Mate

Find yourself a mate who'll throw on the old backpack and *go go go*! Someone who doesn't subscribe to the "American dream" (go to school, get a job, get married, make babies, buy a bunch of shit along the way, die in a strange place surrounded by strangers), but lives with passion (see the quote on Day 23). Someone who doesn't succumb to the materialism of our culture ("dumb white kitchen machinery").

Suggested Kerouactivity:

List 5 places you've never visited but wish you could. Ask your significant other to go to one of them with you this coming weekend. Decide what you're going to do for the rest of your life based on his/ her answer.

DAY 8

Today's Kerouaction:
On Watching Television

Disconnect from the Master Switch! Think of the time you spend sitting on your ass in front of the television! All television does is make us think we are poor, fat, and stupid. And we are none of these – they are only meaningless labels. Go talk to real people if you need connection or information or entertainment! Or, to borrow a popular slogan: kill your television.[18]

Suggested Kerouactivity:

List the television shows you typically watch. Add up the hours per week it requires. Next week, don't watch any of them and commit that amount of time to a hike near water.

---

18   Someone reading this is going to say "But, Rick, *you* watch television." How do you *know* that? Are you with me right now? And so what if I did, or am, or will? This isn't about me, it's about you.

DAY 9

Today's Kerouaction: On Freedom

To quote the movie, *Harley Davidson and the Marlboro Man*, "It's better to be dead and cool than alive and uncool." To wit, when you are out sleeping under the stars, and no one on earth knows where you are, and your life-alienating cell phone is either turned off or, better, not with you, you can experience a rare feeling: freedom. Freedom is one of the key principles behind Kerouactions. It is so important that a little – or perhaps even a lot – of physical discomfort pales in comparison to the feeling that one is at all times and in all situations able to make a choice! The Kerouaction? Live free or die (with thanks to New Hampshire)! Right now, go up to the first person you see and give them $5.00. Tell them a book you are reading told you to do it. Or perhaps your sense of freedom tells you to tell me to take a hike. Great! You are *free* to choose! But always remember that. Do not blame your parents, your past, your mate, your children, events, places, or anything else for your troubles. You *choose*! Freedom....

Suggested Kerouactivity:

Get "Live Free or Die" tattooed somewhere on your body.

DAY 10

Today's Kerouaction:
On Freedom and Materialism

Divest yourself of material goods except for what is absolutely necessary! Here is a rule of thumb to follow: be able to fit everything you own into a backpack (preferably canvas – see Day 28). That is freedom. I often operationalize this to another scale: be able to fit everything you own into your car or truck or whatever vehicle you own. Now that would not be a true Kerouaction, since he avoided vehicle ownership and rarely drove. But he would also say, "Be yourself." And so if you own a vehicle, great. Be able to fit everything you own in it. Jack would find that meritorious, especially in this era of consumerism run amok.[19]

Suggested Kerouactivity:

Write down 7 things you own that you could live without. Pick one and give it away.

---

19   My 27-year-old son recently moved from California to Maine (and back) with all his earthly possessions in a pick-up truck and a small U-Haul trailer. Right on!

DAY 11

Today's Kerouaction: On Compassion

Kerouac would advise being careful about judging others for how they live. That is, while he would advocate forsaking "white kitchen machinery" (a metaphor for the materialism he saw growing in America), he would also caution against judging those who aspire to that kind of life. A paradox? No. As he points out, compassion is the heart of Buddhism.

Suggested Kerouactivity:

Find a definition for compassion from a Buddhist source and write it here.

DAY 12

Today's Kerouaction:
On Resisting What Is

The essential teaching of all spiritual disciplines is that it is our resistance to "what is" that causes suffering. Whatever is, is. This is the second of the Four Noble Truths of Buddhism. Another way to say it: the cause of suffering is attachment and forgetting that nothing is permanent. For more on this, check out the Buddhist writings referenced on Day 5 and *The Power of Now* by Eckhart Tolle.

But what's the Kerouaction? Surrender to the present moment, over and over and over and over . . . .

Suggested Kerouactivity:

Sit still for 10 minutes and don't do anything. Write about what that was like for you.

DAY 13

Today's Kerouaction:
On The Illusion of Things

Kerouac's studies of Buddhism left him feeling even more separated from family members. It is difficult if not impossible to explain the illusion of things to someone who has not read or studied Buddhism, and doing so is especially frustrating since it makes so much sense once one embraces the concept. So, the Kerouaction recommended here is twofold. First, know that nothing exists short of your "mindstuff" about it, and so act accordingly! That is, do not attach to material things! Second, expect that explaining this to the uninitiated will be frustrating at best. Better to just live it, and let your example do the teaching, than to try and explain, especially to a Westerner, that nothing exists except by our thinking about it.

Suggested Kerouactivity:

This section left intentionally empty.

DAY 14

Today's Kerouaction:
On Dogs Being Wiser Than Their Masters

Spiritual teacher and author Eckhart Tolle says in *The Power of Now* (1999) that he has known several Zen masters in his life: all cats.[20] Likewise, Kerouac points out that our egos and our intellect get in the way of enlightenment. Look to animals for clues on being. Or little children. Hmmmm .... Become as little children? A very famous man is credited with saying that a couple thousand years ago. Perhaps he studied the dharma?

Suggested Kerouactivity:

Find a cat or a dog and watch them "be" for 10 minutes without any mental images or comments.

---

20   As I edit this page on May 31, 2007, it occurs to me that a couple of days ago a friend, Heidi, gave me a little plaque with this quote on it: "If cats could talk, they wouldn't." Which reminds me of an interchange credited to Winston Churchill. A woman said to him that if she were his wife, she would poison his coffee. He replied, "If you were my wife, I'd drink it."

DAY 15

Today's Kerouaction: On Spiritual Power

When a problem faces you, become still and pay attention to what your inner voice, your insight, your Buddha nature tells you. Kerouac tried to write from what he called his "native mind." That is, to write his thoughts without refereeing them between thought and paper. In the same way, learn to trust your gut without analyzing what it is telling you. Meditation will strengthen your ability to do this, and for instruction on how to "sit" – or practice "zazen" in Buddhist terms – read *Still the Mind: An Introduction to Meditation* by Alan Watts (2000). There are many excellent Buddhist authors. Watts just happens to be one of my favorites.[21] Sitting zazen is the recommended Kerouaction here. And remember what Marianne Williamson (1996) says, "Our deepest fear is not that we are inadequate. Our deepest fear is that we are powerful beyond measure."

Suggested Kerouactivity:

Write down a problem you have. What Kerouaction is necessary?

---

21   Growth is a curious thing. Since writing this entry (on 3/14/05 and it is now 5/31/07), I have changed my opinion about the value of systems or methods – zazen being one of many – for understanding the truth. Read some J. Krishnamurti if you want to know more.

DAY 16

Today's Kerouaction: On Action v. Words

I said in the very first sentence of this book's introduction that Jack Kerouac was a man of action. That was part of his essence, and perhaps why he resonated with Buddhism. Paradoxically, while the average lay person thinks of Buddhists sitting around meditating and doing nothing, in fact that is not the point. The sitting *is* something. And it is nothing. But "talking" about Buddhism, about sitting, about the law of impermanence, etc., is missing the "experiencing" aspect of it.[22] The experiencing of "now." Fully. And Jack knew that before he ever discovered Buddhism.

So what is the Kerouaction here? *Do something!* Stop sitting around planning and thinking and analyzing and go take a hike, make love, get drunk, write a book, plant a garden, talk with friends, *something!* Now. That is the only time anything happens. Now. Everything you remember happening in the past happened in the now. Everything you anticipate happening in the future will happen in the now. Thank you, Eckhart Tolle, for making that clear to the Western mind.[23] So "now" is all there is, and all there ever is. So whatever you are doing, eve if it is nothing, *experience* it! Fully. Enough said.

Suggested Kerouactivity:

Words written here would be an abomination.

---

22   Alan Watts called this the "stink of Zen."
23   And thanks to Dan Millman, too, for his *Peaceful Warrior* writings, although he's a little too cutesy for me. I did like the movie, though, and Nick Nolte was well-cast as Socrates.

DAY 17

Today's Kerouaction: On Breakfast

Kerouac routinely detailed what his characters ate. From this, we can ascertain a certain "beat diet,"[24] so to speak. For breakfast tomorrow, make some home fries (from scratch, of course, starting with fresh potatoes). When they are done, throw in some eggs and cook them right up with the potatoes, scrambling the whole thing together. Enjoy your "slumgullion."

Suggested Kerouactivity:

When you next make slumgullion to enjoy, write down the date on this page. If you modify the directions, this might be a good spot to document the recipe.

---

24   See also Days 1, 19, 24, 52, 54, & 57.

DAY 18

Today's Kerouaction: On Appearances

Abandon materialism. Forget appearances. Live simply. Raise your own vegetables. Live with cats. Discover your Buddha nature.

Tomorrow, throw out something you have been hanging on to for years. Throw it in the trash and laugh. Or give it to someone! That would be even better for the environment. You won't miss it and you surely don't "need" it. What do you need? Little. We all need the same things. Among them are shelter, food, connection, and spirituality. What does that "thing" you are going to throw away have to do with any of that?

Suggested Kerouactivity:

In the space below, make a list of 10 things you are going to give away or sell and check them off as you do so.

DAY 19

Today's Kerouaction:
On Food for the Road

More on the "beat diet"[25]: Ry-Krisp crackers, cheddar cheese, salami. Throw that in your backpack and take off for parts unknown. Or known. No matter, as long as you *go go go*!

Suggested Kerouactivity:

Use this page to list all the "beat foods" you read about in Kerouac's books.

---

25   See also Days 1, 17, 24, 52, 54, & 57.

DAY 20

Today's Kerouaction:
On Walking Meditation

Japhy's advice to Smith (Kerouac) echoes that of many Buddhist teachers who advocate "practicing" not only "on the cushion" but also during other activities, such as walking. Thich Nhat Hanh (1996) wrote an entire book on the subject: *The Long Road Turns to Joy: A Guide to Walking Meditation*. The spiritual benefits of mindfulness accrue no matter the activity, of course, and one can practice anywhere, anytime. Mowing the grass comes to mind as one example. So, whether you are hiking or mowing the lawn, practice.[26]

Suggested Kerouactivity:

Jiddu Krishnamurti would likely disagree with the advice above. Read something by him and see if you can explain why.

---

26   Better yet, practice as J. Krishnamurti advises and meet each moment anew, with choiceless awareness. All teachers, gurus, systems, methods, mantras, etc. are keeping you from the truth.

DAY 21

Today's Kerouaction: On Impermanence

This too shall pass. That pretty much sums up Buddhism, especially the "law of impermanence." Or as they say about the weather in Tioga County, PA: If you don't like it, wait a minute. It will change. (They say that in Maine, too.)

Nothing good stays. Nothing bad lasts. Nothing. Why experience any single moment with less than total wonder and joy and appreciation? The Kerouaction here is to stop your whining and keep going! Love every second of this life, whether it's your preference or not. It's okay not to like your situation. But as Rumi says, welcome it![27]

Suggested Kerouactivity:

Identify what's going on in your life right now that you hope will last, or that you hope will end. See your attachment to such things and how it prevents you from enjoying now.

---

27   It's beyond my ken in which of Rumi's writings I read that. Sorry for the scholarship gap.

DAY 22

Today's Kerouaction: On Gifts

When you give someone a gift, give it to them from your heart! That may mean – and often does mean – creating the gift (versus buying it). Smith (Kerouac) gives Japhy an original saying,[28] with Buddhist overtones, which can be easily carried[29] and referenced. And it was a gift of "words," Kerouac's true gift to the world, and to Japhy. That is what I mean by giving from your heart. What is it that can uniquely come, that can only come, from you to another?

Suggested Kerouactivity:

Write down the next time you can think of when you will likely be getting someone a gift. Decide – right now – what you will give them that can only come from you.

---

28   A little piece of paper about the size of a thumbnail on which Kerouac had written, "MAY YOU USE THE DIAMONDCUTTER OF MERCY" (Kerouac, 1976b, p. 215).
29   In the spirit of traveling light and unencumbered by material goods – see Days 6 and 10.

DAY 23

Today's Kerouaction: On Friends

Perhaps the most oft-quoted passage from Kerouac is in *On The Road* (1976):

> The only people for me are the mad ones, the ones who are mad to live, mad to talk, mad to be saved, desirous of everything at the same time, the ones who never yawn or say a commonplace thing, but burn, burn, burn like fabulous yellow roman candles exploding like spiders across the stars and in the middle you see the blue centerlight pop and everybody goes "Awww!" (p. 8).

The above passage refers to Dean Moriarty (real-life Kerouac friend Neal Cassady) and Carlo Marx (real-life Kerouac friend Allen Ginsburg). Moriarty and Sal Paradise (Kerouac) are the main characters in *On The Road*, a novel which arguably established Kerouac as a literary force and, some would say, forever changed the look of the American novel.

But that is literary gobbledy-gook and not the point. It has been said that one is judged by the company one keeps. It is not too much of a stretch to say that one is influenced by the company one keeps. So look to the company you keep. Are the people you choose to associate with unpredictable? Passionate? Rambunctious? Or predictable? Boring? Complacent? Decide which you want to be. Then choose your friends. Wisely. As Mary Oliver asks in her poem, "The Summer Day": "What will you do with your one wild and passionate life?"

I say, for one thing, hang out with people who live on the edge. Otherwise, you'll be taking up too much space.

Suggested Kerouactivity:

Think of someone who you would love to hang out with but don't because of what other people might say. Come on. You can think of one. Write down that person's name right here. You know what to do next.

DAY 24

Today's Kerouaction: On Food

On Sal Paradise's (Kerouac's) first trip across America to the glorious west, he often ate apple pie and ice cream. One can imagine the part of the midwest where the apple pie and ice cream, at the time, were the best in the world: fresh, scrumptious, addictive. And it got better the deeper he went into Iowa. So, make a trip to your nearest diner and order up some apple pie and ice cream.[30] Think about Jack while you enjoy it, and welcome to another recommended item in the "beat diet."[31]

Suggested Kerouactivity:

Take this book with you when you enjoy your pie and ice cream. When you're done, wipe your fingers on this page as evidence. Or if you don't want to do that, describe the person who served you.

---

30   Or whatever is close. If you are in Gardiner, ME, and you're at the world-famous A1 Diner, they may not have plain old apple pie. But they have pies you'll love and they go great with ice cream. Plus it is a beat place for sure!
31   See also Days 1, 17, 19, 52, 54, & 57.

DAY 25

Today's Kerouaction: On Hitchhiking

Start hitchhiking to get places. And no, it is *not* illegal everywhere (check out the Internet for specifics). Just highly dangerous! Even if it is illegal, that just makes it more beat: Kerouac and his beat friends broke the law regularly! Second, other people matter. When someone is kind enough to pick you up, make an effort in conversation so that they might pick up someone else some day. Tell them an interesting story about your travels. Anything so their experience doesn't turn them off from picking up hitchhikers. Reinforce their behavior. Third, when you're off to somewhere, *go go go*. Don't spend the night in hotels between point A and point B. Start at point A and travel nonstop to point B. You'll save money and time, and you'll have a much more intense journey.

Suggested Kerouactivity:

Write down the names of 5 places you are going to visit by hitchhiking in the next year.

DAY 26

Today's Kerouaction: On Enthusiasm

Seek out the enthusiastic, the passionate people along your journey (see Day 23). That will go a long way toward preventing your life from becoming "commonplace," and keep you on the beat path.

Who is it in your circle of friends that oozes enthusiasm? If you can think of some, cherish them. If you can't, rethink your friends. Is there someone you consider merely an acquaintance who lives passionately? Maybe they could be more than just an acquaintance. How might Kerouac go about making a friend of him or her?

Suggested Kerouactivity:

Magically, this space is for Crystal. No assignment is possible.

DAY 27

Today's Kerouaction:
On the "Beat" Character

"Beatness" is not necessarily a condition defined by where one lives, or by what one wears. It is a way of being. Cowboys can be beat. That means you can be, too. What action will you take today toward beatness? Here's a suggestion: at dawn tomorrow, walk the streets or the roads or somewhere you'll be seen by passers-by. Let them wonder about you. Why are you walking there at this time of day? Maybe they will think you look "beat." Hallelujah!

Suggested Kerouactivity:

Describe a beat character you see walking around where you live. What can you learn from this person about beatness?

DAY 28

Today's Kerouaction: On Clothing

In Jack's kindness to Eddie, a fellow hitchhiker, we get a hint at a piece of clothing one might choose in order to follow the beat path: wool plaid shirts. In other places Kerouac calls them "lumberjack shirts." You know the kind: red, plaid, the kind Paul Bunyan probably wore. Many pictures of Jack confirm his love of the wool plaid shirt. Now it is possible that Kerouac would approve a wool "blend" or even cotton. We don't know for sure. We do know that while cotton flannel shirts feel better on our skin, there is nothing like wool for durability and warmth. Get over the itchiness. Use it as a meditation. When you feel the itch, it can remind you to be fully aware in the present moment.

One also gets a hint at the kind of bag to use in carrying one's possessions while on the road: canvas. The hell with all this newfangled ripstop breathable nylon earth-polluting resource-depleting synthetic crap!

Suggested Kerouactivity:

Get yourself a good old-fashioned canvas bag. Land's End still makes them, don't they? Or how about the Boy Scouts? Or how about visiting your nearest used clothing store[32] and scrounging around? That is almost always a worthwhile idea and you never know: you might find a wool plaid shirt to boot. And while you're at it, drop off something you haven't worn or used in a year.

---

32   Or "vintage apparel" store, the euphemism for used clothes, according to George Carlin.

DAY 29

Today's Kerouaction: On Generosity

Riding on the back of a flatbed truck driven by two young blond farmers from Minnesota who were picking up every hitchhiker possible on a whirlwind trip to L.A., Kerouac freely shares his cigarettes with Gene and his boy, two fellow hobo travelers. Another traveler, Montana Slim, had his own but never passed the pack. It seems that part of the beat way is to recognize a fellow traveler when you see one and take a "what's-mine-is-yours and vice versa" attitude, with a hope of reciprocity (or karma?). Besides, shirts and cigarettes and booze are just material goods, comforts along the way, nice to have but not necessary, not "IT" (more on "IT" later – see Day 85).

Suggested Kerouactivity:

Next time you are at the bar, buy a round for the house. Or next time you go through a toll booth, pay the toll for the person behind you. Describe the reaction on this page.

DAY 30

Today's Kerouaction: On Fun

Read about "pisscall" on p. 31 of *On The Road* (1976).[33] Isn't that a great and fun passage? I wrote something I thought was scholarly and profound for this entry, but decided after reading it that it was best said like this: goof on your friends whenever possible and pee wherever you happen to be when the urge strikes.[34] That is, live! And have fun while you're at it. If your friends can't take a goof, get some new ones. If you can't bring yourself to pee except in dumb white bathroom machinery, perhaps you might ask yourself why.

Suggested Kerouactivity:

Go outside and pee. Now.

---

33   Sorry. I just couldn't leave you to your own devices for finding this one because you absolutely *have* to read this passage as part of your beat education.
34   Or pee on a jellyfish sting to ease the pain (a gratuitous pop culture movie reference).

DAY 31

Today's Kerouaction:
On Finding Someone for the Night

Sal (Kerouac) wasn't successful with a pickup ploy in Cheyenne, but it echoes the advice given me by two hucksters on Bourbon Street in New Orleans during April 2004 wherein they advised me to be unbelievably direct and specific when approaching women. Now their approach was a bit bawdier (and certainly less romantic – see my disclaimer below) than Kerouac's, and decorum prevents me from detailing it here, but suffice to say that the direct approach is statistically sound, and I have confirmed that in practice and by some informal canvassing of others. Sooner or later, if you ask enough times, someone is going to say, "Yes."

The Kerouaction here is simple. If you are seeking the "company" of another for the night, ask. Doing it via a poem scribbled on the check in a restaurant is one way, or you can go right up to someone – as did Todd and Tommy in New Orleans – and tell them in graphic detail what you would like to do. Try it. You may be surprised by the results. A disclaimer: I'm not anti-romantic by any means; in fact, I rather think the "poem-on-the-back-of-the-nearest-piece-of-paper" method is a good cross between directness and romance. It depends on what you say in the poem, of course. I know what Todd and Tommy would write. Oh my . . . .

Suggested Kerouactivity:

While not very spontaneous, use this space to draft a beat poem you might use next time you are in need of an "icebreaker" with someone.

DAY 32

Today's Kerouaction:
On the Rules of the Road

When you are "on the road," keep these suggestions in mind: 1) Keep moving. Do not "dawdle" long in places. *Go go go!* 2) Save some money for later in the trip, despite the temptation to spend it all on drinks in order to "make" a girl as Sal (Kerouac) did with the sullen girl in one passage.[35] 3) If you are going to fool around with someone, avoid the sullen types. Better to go without.

Suggested Kerouactivity:

Write down 10 rules you live by. Break half of them by the end of next week.

---

35   Perhaps a handwritten poem on a meal check would have sufficed? See Day 31.

DAY 33

Today's Kerouaction: On Taking Action

Sal's (Kerouac's) delight at actually making it to Denver (well, *almost* at the point I'm focusing on) is infectious and serves to teach us the power of acting out a desire. William Blake said, "Better to strangle an infant in its cradle than nurse unacted desires." If you desire to do something, do it. I might suggest that you refrain from activities that cause harm to others. But the point here is that you have choices! You do not have to live where you live. You do not have to be with the person you are with. You do not have to stay stuck in that job. You don't. It's your choice. Take action. Then you can say, "Damn! damn! damn! I actually [fill in your desired action here]!

Suggested Kerouactivity:

This space is for venting all the regrets you have about things you could have done and didn't.

DAY 34

Today's Kerouaction: On Wow!

Kerouac occasionally employs the interjection "Wow!" to express his delight at something. It's a timeless expression, still in use today, so feel free to use it when you have done something or seen something wonderful and exciting and passion-filled (which will happen a lot if you follow the beat path). But save it for those times. Please.

Suggested Kerouactivity:

Add to the following list other beat interjections you could be using in your daily discourse:

> *Wow!*
> *Yair!*

DAY 35

Today's Kerouaction: On Parties

Partying beat style involves 3 things: the opposite sex (and plenty of them), alcohol (drugs, too, although they are not mentioned in the scene I'm referencing), and simple food (hey, what's wrong with beans and franks?).

Given the above, and given that there is no need for music in order to dance, stop your extensive party planning and throw a beat party. Read the preparation for this particular party and you will see that it is thrown in an old abandoned miner's shack that they had to spend all day cleaning. Whatever your place looks like, heat up some beans and franks, lay in a big supply of beer and whiskey, invite everyone you can think of, and party on, dude.[36]

Suggested Kerouactivity:

Use the space below to make a list of everyone you are going to invite to your beat party.

---

36   Another movie reference for you to figure out.

DAY 36

Today's Kerouaction: On Bars

I quite understand the concept of local bars and regulars and the latter's disdain for nonlocals, or "tourists" as Kerouac says they were called in this passage.[37] So when you are hitting the bars in the next new place you hitchhike – which is a suggested action – expect to be held in disregard if you frequent the "local bar," versus a more chain-type variety. Or, if *you* are a local, perhaps you might keep this passage in mind when sitting at the bar with your friends and a stranger or two walk in. They may not be tourists. They may be beats. Treat them accordingly.[38]

Suggested Kerouactivity:

Write down the name of the nearest bar to your present location. Plan to practice today's Kerouaction there in the next two weeks.

---

37   Especially as I write this on August 22, 2006, having to date been routinely ignored by locals at the local watering hole.
38   Update: I've sort of become a regular at the aforementioned establishment (The Depot in Gardiner, Maine), which has adopted the motto, "Regulars rule."

DAY 37

Today's Kerouaction: On Pick-Up Lines

"What do you want out of life?" may be the quintessential beat pick-up line. This question has two purposes. One is obvious and I don't need to belabor it here. But the other is to probe for depth. That is, has this person formulated a larger purpose? Asked the big questions? Decided to live passionately?[39]

Suggested Kerouactivity:

Craft an alternative pick-up line for future reference.

---

39   See Day 31 for additional advice.

DAY 38

Today's Kerouaction: On Courting

Whereas the beat generation – and especially the hippie generation it spawned – has a reputation for meaningless, casual sex, it would seem that the "king of the beats" advises that there is more to it than that. Granted, we might be talking about an uncommitted, "one-night stand," but even within that context we ought to attempt a soul-to-soul connection in addition to the physical. This may explain the pick-up line which is the subject of Day 37. Depending on the situation, of course, this line may be seen as merely a pick-up line, even if delivered with sincerity. Timing is important as well as delivery. Find your own way to get into "real straight talk about souls" when you are "courting" – either short-term or long-term. It will reap beat dividends, because you are after "IT" (see Day 85).

Suggested Kerouactivity:

Write a beat love poem here. You never know when it might come in handy!

DAY 39

Today's Kerouaction: On Nicknames

My whole life I have been saying things like, "Yo, what's up?" but I never knew until I discovered Kerouac that it was an appellation.[40] I remember this phrase from my youth in the early 1960s, making it more or less a "hippie" term, but it's certainly possible it was inspired by the beats and perhaps specifically by the passage at hand. No matter. It's a stalwart nickname and worthy of use with each other. I recommend it.

Suggested Kerouactivity:

Write down some beat nicknames you use or could use with your friends.

---

40   Or, as Crystal taught me the other day, a "hypocorism." What a great word!

DAY 40

Today's Kerouaction: On Livelihoods

A beat policeman? This seeming paradox – someone who typifies the "anti-establishment" lifestyle becoming a law enforcement type – indeed tells us that it is okay to use the system to beat it. That is, if money is a necessary strategy for doing those things you want to do, and you are at a point where doing something beat to earn money is not happening, it's okay to earn money doing pretty much anything. Even being a policeman. I bet Kerouac looked at it as a necessary evil, an ironic act, a way to take advantage of the system. So if you can earn a living writing or playing music, go for it. If you can't, consider homelessness and mooching. As a last resort, get a job. Any kind will do as long as you don't let it kill your soul.

Suggested Kerouactivity:

Make a list of five ideal beat jobs. Find a newspaper and see if any listings match entries on your list.

DAY 41

Today's Kerouaction: On Stealing

Sal Paradise (Kerouac) talks about stealing food from the cafeteria barracks where he served as a guard. His co-worker and shack-mate, Remi, justified it by saying, "Paradise, I have told you several times what President Truman said, *we must cut down on the cost of living*" (Kerouac, 1976a, pp. 70-71).

Now I am not advocating breaking the law. But "helping oneself" to those things necessary for survival – food and clothing, for example – is not beyond the beat way. So if it's a matter of survival – and realizing that stealing can have consequences you may not enjoy (e.g., like jail) – "on the road" and traveling light, you might think about a little pilfering. I recommend that it be from those who won't miss it (like certain mega-corporations that weren't in existence during Kerouac's time).

Suggested Kerouactivity:

Devise a plan for survival on the road without any money.

DAY 42

Today's Kerouaction: On Exploring

Where to start? First, sunbathe naked. (And do not use sunscreen – *that* is what is causing all the skin cancer, *not* the sun. Your skin needs the sun. Kerouac never mentions sunscreen one time in all of his writing, and he didn't die of skin cancer and he was outside a lot.[41]) Second, take risks and explore things that might be interesting. You might pass by buildings or boats or cars each day of your life and never think about exploring them.[42] Think about it! Third, see the romantic in those old cars, boats, buildings. Who lived there? Worked there? Loved there? Died there? Think on these things when you encounter the remnants of yesterday. Finally, read some Jack London. He was a huge influence on Kerouac. Start tomorrow. Or *now* would be even better.

Suggested Kerouactivity:

Get a copy of Jack London's (1903) <u>Call of the Wild</u>. Turn to the page corresponding with the day of the month you were born plus 42. Read that page and think about it without accepting or denying what it says. Formulate an action based on that page. Take the action. Describe the outcome here.

---

41   I know, I know – it's the depleted ozone layer causing more skin cancer. To which I reply: Barbara Streisand.
42   For example, there is a fountain in the mall in downtown Bar Harbor, ME, that begs to be bouldered.

DAY 43

Today's Kerouaction: On Best Laid Plans

This is one of the most important Kerouactions in this book: See America from the road! You can still do it – there is time! Get a copy of *On The Road* and use it as a map. Visit all the places Kerouac visited. Do not drive. Hitchhike or catch the bus. In this way you will get the full experience of America, meeting people and enjoying as-yet-unknown adventures along the way. When you get to the end, go back. That's okay. It's the journey, the process, that matters – not the outcome! And that is why this entry is called, "On Best Laid Plans." Even though Kerouac describes his first trip to the west coast as disastrous, it's all good as long as you are following your heart and living each moment and staying on the *go go go*. Kerouac wrote a best-selling book based on his trip! How disastrous is that?

Suggested Kerouactivity:

Attach a map of the United States to your wall. Take 5 paces back. Close your eyes. Throw a dart. Circle the nearest village, town, or city to where the dart landed. Remove the dart. Take down the map. Fold it and put it in your backpack with the other "road essentials" (see Days 19, 28, 57, & 75). Go go go to the circled location as fast and as beat as you can. Leave today. Don't tell anyone you're going. Write about your adventures (but not just in this space – it's too small). Repeat as necessary.

DAY 44

Today's Kerouaction: On Clothing

Buy your clothes used. They are cheaper that way and it is better for the environment (you're welcome, Edward Abbey). Goodwill, Salvation Army, mom-and-pop consignment stores, church thrift shops – they're all beat sources for your clothing.

Suggested Kerouactivity:

Raid your closet or dresser or wherever you keep your clothing and set aside all the clothing you have not worn in a year. Take it to the nearest used clothing store and donate it all. While you're there, look for your next backpack (see Day 28). You can buy clothes if you want, but what's the point after just getting rid of a bunch? No writing assignment today. Take a break.

DAY 45

Today's Kerouaction: On Women

Kerouac sets forth for our discernment the archetypal woman's physical characteristics (straight true breasts, delicious flanks, long lustrous black hair, and blue eyes). And, we see from his musings that it is not unusual – as it is not unusual for Jim Carrey's character in the movie *Eternal Sunshine of the Spotless Mind* – to fall in love instantly and with pretty much every beautiful woman we see.[43] Perhaps one might want to take the advice from Day 31 (re: Tommy and Todd from New Orleans) and not let such opportunities pass?

Suggested Kerouactivity:

Next time you see the archetypal beat beauty, walk right up and tell her you love her. Write down her reaction here.[44]

---

43   I cannot speak for Kerouac on whether this translates across gender, but I suspect it is a male trait.
44   Either gender can try this one, of course, but we don't have an archetypal male description, unless it's Dean Moriarty (Neal Cassidy). I guess a female undertaking this assignment might use Dean as the archtype. For a real life example, think of actor Thomas Jane.

DAY 46

Today's Kerouaction: On Taking Action[45]

Once Kerouac got on a bus and saw a Mexican girl sitting alone, and he finally struck up the nerve to talk to her.[46] The point of this entry is this: act! Do something! Anything! The worst thing you can do is nothing, because then you will be on your deathbed with the worst regrets of all: regrets about missed opportunities. Or as John Greenleaf Whittier points out in his poem, "Maud Muller":

> For of all sad words of tongue or pen,
> The saddest are these: "It might have been!"[47]

Suggested Kerouactivity:

Do your assignment for Day 45 and then read "Maud Muller." Then, write a poem in this space. Writing and reading poetry is a beat thing to do. Plus, it's an action![48]

---

45   For a similar entry, see Day 16.
46   Because of the copyright police, you will have to pick up a copy of *On The Road* to find out what happens. No big deal, because outcome is not the point of this entry.
47   I was turned on to this passage from an episode of the TV show, *The Equalizer*, starring Edward Woodward. That show had some very beat regular characters.
48   FYI, watching television is *not* an action.

DAY 47

Today's Kerouaction: On Boredom

I can hear it now: "There's nothing to do here. There's nowhere to go on a date. We're bored." Well, a smart person once told me that only boring people get bored.[49] So grab a cheap bottle of wine and go sit out under the stars and drink and talk. It doesn't have to be in a railroad yard, although that is recommended for its symbolism (*go go go*) and because Kerouac hopped a lot of trains in his day as a means of transportation. Outside and free are the keys. How about the empty high school football stadium? How about on top of the nearest mountain peak you can see from where you are standing right now? No mountain peaks? What's the highest thing you can see from where you are? Find your way atop it! With a bottle. And your sweetheart. Your sweetheart doesn't think that sounds like fun? Find a new sweetheart. Cheers!

Suggested Kerouactivity:

Find and buy a bottle of cheap wine. Kerouac bought a quart of California port for 35 cents. If that were in 1957, it would be worth $2.58 in 2007 dollars (according to the online inflation calculator I used). Don't go higher than $2.58! You know what to do with the wine.

---

49   A year after writing this passage, I heard the speaker at Crystal's son's graduation ceremony say that bored people are boring and interested people are interesting.

DAY 48

Today's Kerouaction: On Movies

Forget the clock and stay up all night. That's number one. Second, even in town you can find places to hang *outside*. Third, and the main point of this entry, it's perfectly beat to seize on a phrase (or phrases) from a movie or book and repeat it (or them) aloud endlessly.[50] For example, I often say, "You are not your job," or "You are not your car." These are references to *Fight Club*. When you invoke a movie reference, don't explain yourself unless asked. Fourth, find a sweetheart who accepts you the way you are, who doesn't see you as a "project." That's the kind of non-clingy love to seek after.

Suggested Kerouactivity:

Watch <u>Fight Club</u>. *Tonight. Pick a line (Suggestion: "You're the all-singing, all-dancing crap of the world." – Tyler Durden). Write it down below. Memorize it. Use it endlessly for a few weeks.*

---

50   Kerouac was reciting lines from John Steinbeck's *Of Mice and Men*.

DAY 49

Today's Kerouaction: On Sleep

Kerouac mentions sleeping until noon. Regardless of the weather or what your lover is doing, sleep in if that is what trips your trigger on any given day. You have a job, a time clock, a boss, responsibilities? Sleep in anyway.

Suggested Kerouactivity:

Zzzzzzzzzzzzzzzzzzzzzzzzzzzzzzzzzzzzzzzzzz….

DAY 50

Today's Kerouaction: On Priorities

Kerouac prioritized activities. For example, which is better – time spent working or drinking? This is a beat generation no-brainer. Work is to be avoided whenever possible, and when given the choice between work and a bottle, the bottle wins every time. When you can't afford a bottle, work a little bit and make enough money to buy one. Drink up. Repeat the process. Any questions?

Suggested Kerouactivity:

List your current priorities here (e.g., family, work, religion, country, play, drinking, etc.). Next to your list, write them again re-organized in beat fashion. Compare the two. What changes can you make to your priorities to make them more beatific?

DAY 51

Today's Kerouaction:
On Interconnectedness

We're born, we die, and in between we experience – with everyone else – life! We're all interconnected by the common human experience. Or, as I learned in high school French class from Madame Griggs:

> The ins and outs
> The ups and downs
> The comings and goings
> Of life and death
> Are here to stay.

It's kind of a Zen thing, you know? Enjoy the ride and the knowledge that you are not alone on it, no matter what happens!

Suggested Kerouactivity:

Strike up a conversation with the next person you run into whose name you don't know. Need an icebreaker? Tell them you have to meet five new people for a project you're doing. If they ask what project, tell them you are trying to become beat. That might get an interaction going!

DAY 52

Today's Kerouaction: On Food

Still more on the "beat diet."[51] Kerouac talks of eating tacos and mashed pinto beans rolled in tortillas. Mexican food is a staple, probably for two big reasons: it's cheap and it's tasty. But don't go to Taco Bell![52] Beatness and corporate food chains are not complementary. Make your own Mexican meal at home or go to an "authentic" Mexican restaurant.

Suggested Kerouactivity:

To really experience the beat diet, get on the road tomorrow bright and early and head for Mexico. No stopping until you get there, and the first thing you eat "in-country" has to be tacos and mashed pinto beans rolled in tortillas.

---

51   See also Days 1, 17, 19, 24, 54, & 57.
52   Although my friend Keith, who's a pretty beat character, swears by bean burritos at *Taco Bell* as cheap good food.

DAY 53

Today's Kerouaction:
On Hope and Procrastination

Kerouac speaks of his love's frequent use of the phrase *mañana*, saying everything would be all right tomorrow. Hope and procrastination? How do those two concepts fit together? Easily! It's a very beat thing to do to procrastinate (i.e., put off until tomorrow what you could do today), but it's also a very beat thing to have hope. So while you're procrastinating (hopefully avoiding work or some other such life-alienating drudgery in favor of sex or drinking or just gazing at the stars with your sweetheart), you're hoping for good things to come. Whatever they may be. It's all good. Especially when you are procrastinating.

Suggested Kerouactivity:

The very next time you owe someone money by a certain date (e.g., a bill), don't pay it until at least a month late. If you never pay bills late, this is a very important thing for you to do as part of becoming beat.[53] *If you're always or frequently late with payments, this assignment is moot. Congratulations on already being a beat.*

---

53   The other day, one of my college students wrote in a journal that she had never in her life turned in an assignment late. I told her to try it. She said she might. How cool is that?

DAY 54

Today's Kerouaction: On Food

Kerouac borrows a bicycle and pedals to the crossroads grocery store to buy food: cooked spaghetti and meatballs, bread, butter, coffee, and cake. Why own a vehicle (human-powered or otherwise) when you can borrow one?[54] And when you shop for groceries, patronize the "Mom & Pop" store on the corner (if you can find one in this corporate-bagging mega-chain environment – mine is called Day's in Belgrade Lakes, Maine). Now, I have to be honest and say that the biggest reason I included this "beat diet" entry is that Chef Boyardee canned spaghetti and meatballs has been one of my favorite foods since childhood. Mmmmmmm . . . .

Suggested Kerouactivity:

For dinner tonight, have Chef Boyardee canned spaghetti and meatballs.[55]

---

54   This goes for fiddles, too. John Hartford used to tell of a fiddler he knew who never owned a fiddle: "He'd play on yours." Listen to his CD, *Hamilton Ironworks*.

55   For other beat diet ideas, see Days 1, 17, 19, 24, 52, & 57.

DAY 55

Today's Kerouaction: On Entertainment

You can't be far from a cemetery, no matter where you live.[56] So visit your nearest one, climb a tree, and sing a song. "Blue Skies" if you know it. Otherwise, your favorite song will do. See, it doesn't cost much of anything to find entertainment!

Speaking of cemeteries, I have started visiting the gravesites of my favorite writers. While there, I read some of their work and drink a shot of Bushmills (my father's favorite whiskey). So far I've carried out this routine at the graves of Kerouac, Robert Frost, and Edwin Arlington Robinson (I have loved "Richard Cory" since high school and have even memorized it). You might want to adopt this routine. Maybe you could refine it, figuring out the author's favorite drink and taking that along.

Suggested Kerouactivity:

Write down the words to "Blue Skies" below and begin memorizing.

---

56   Or don't live, for that matter. If you're homeless – which, by the way, is a very beat way to live when it's by choice – pick the nearest cemetery to where you hang out.

DAY 56

Today's Kerouaction: On Parting

When you part from a significant other – same or opposite sex – what you do at parting is critical. Kerouac describes turning to look at each other after a dozen paces. A parting is something you will likely remember forever. Find a way to make it interesting. Since "love is a duel" (Kerouac, 1976a, p. 101), perhaps turning at a dozen paces is the best way to part with a lover. Or maybe you just walk away backwards looking at each other until you are out of sight. Whatever! Make it memorable.

Suggested Kerouactivity:

I just couldn't muster up an assignment for this one. You'll have to do that on your own. If you come up with something wonderful, drop me a note about it and maybe I'll include it in the reprint.

DAY 57

Today's Kerouaction: On Traveling Food

Few Americans these days would stuff unrefrigerated salami into their backpack for a cross county trek. But it would be the beat way to go. Simple. Effective. Tasty. All this talk of salmonella and other nasties waiting to kill you unless you sanitize and never leave food out and blah blee blah is just so much government propaganda to keep you consuming so the wheels of progress can march on and on and on . . . . Take a risk once in a while and stop believing what the government says.

Suggested Kerouactivity:

Make a salami sandwich right now. Leave it out until tomorrow. Then eat it. You'll feel better. It's the beat diet,[57] you know.

---

57   For other beat diet ideas, see Days 1, 17, 19, 24, 52, & 54.

DAY 58

Today's Kerouaction: On Possessions

When you're traveling the beat way – for example, by hitchhiking or public transportation – you don't need reading material because you can occupy your time "reading the American landscape." If you do want a book, steal it. Then give it away. You don't need possessions. You only think you do. Possessions are not needs. Possessions are strategies to meet needs. What needs of yours does the strategy of possessing things meet? Is there another strategy to meet those same needs?[58] Think about it . . . .

In the meantime, pay attention to what you see out there in the great outdoors every day. You may find you don't need any or as many possessions. Do you have to possess the mountain or the sunset to revel in it?

Suggested Kerouactivity:

List your top ten most prized possessions below. Give one of them away by the end of the month, no strings attached.

---

58   For more on this, see Rosenberg (1999).

DAY 59

Today's Kerouaction: On Barter[59]

You don't need cash for things. You can barter. And you don't need material stuff to barter with either. Can you write or sing a song? Craft a poem? Tell a story? Dig a ditch? Sweep a floor? Those are worth something to someone. Find out who it is! Practice barter whenever you can. It's the beat thing to do.

Oh, I almost forgot the other Kerouactions in the passage about barter: Find a nearsighted girl (or guy). Then you don't have to worry about Red Green's adage: "If they don't find you handsome, at least they can find you handy." And neck a lot. If your mate doesn't like to neck a lot, find a new one.

Suggested Kerouactivity:

Every community seems to have a weekly rag full of classified ads (it's called Uncle Henry's here in Maine). Get a copy and search for ads where people are offering to barter goods or services. See if you can take them up on it. Or if you can't find something about barter, put in an ad offering to barter. Can't afford the ad? See if the publisher will barter. Ha!

---

59   See also Day 99.

DAY 60

Today's Kerouaction:
On the Susquehanna

Being a Pennsylvania boy, and having lived and worked in the Harrisburg area for years (that is where Kerouac walks the Susquehanna in one passage), I was duty-bound to include this entry. Kerouac gives a dead-on balls accurate[60] description of a great river that pretty much cuts Pennsylvania into two parts. But what is the Kerouaction? Simple. Get your butt down to the Susquehanna River near Harrisburg, PA, and do some walking. Walk where Kerouac walked. It's good for the soul. Trust me . . . .

Suggested Kerouactivity:

Get a copy of Thoreau's essay, "On Walking." Remember not to buy it (see Day 58). Read it carefully at least three times and jot down some thoughts below.

---

60   Another movie reference (see Day 48). Can you tell which one?

DAY 61

Today's Kerouaction:
On Obstacles to Going

Dean (Neal Cassady) demonstrates the tenacity with which a beat travels, stopping for nothing, not even an icy windshield. Reading this passage made me think of 3 AM mornings on back roads, traveling home from my girlfriend's house in the thick Pennsylvania fog, with my head out the window trying to see the side of the road by the right front tire and crawling along at a turtle's speed. I guess I was beat and didn't know it! Well, when you have to get somewhere, you have to get somewhere – weather cannot be a deterrent. You just *go go go*.

Suggested Kerouactivity:

Stop reading this book and go somewhere (but keep the book with you). Anywhere. When you get there, turn to any page in this book and perform the Kerouaction (if applicable – if not, turn to another page and do that one).

DAY 62

Today's Kerouaction: On Now

Gilbert K. Chesterton is credited with saying, "The world will never starve for want of wonders, but for want of wonder."[61] Not so with a beat. Every moment is a miracle – as Walt Whitman observed – to be cherished and held in wonder.[62] This perspective is at the heart of zen, and so too at the heart of beatness. Whatever is happening right now, that is all there is – be in wonder at it. Go outside. Close your eyes. Sit quietly. Listen to the sounds. Smell the aromas. Feel the ground under you. Experience the *now*.

Suggested Kerouactivity:

Okay, it's time for a specific reading recommendation. Get a copy of Eckhart Tolle's The Power of Now *(1999) and read it. Skip the parts about the pain body. That is new age bullshit. The rest of it is gold. Of course, it is all just Krishnamurti in a new package suitable for this hyperactive, sound-bite culture. So if the latter is you, go with Tolle. If the latter is not, go with Krishnamurti (see References).*

---

61   Forgive my lack of scholarship on the source, but check the Internet if you're interested.
62   Again, pardon my lack of scholarship. I saw it on a magnet, okay? Probably from quotablecards.com, a very cool and probably beat company.

DAY 63

Today's Kerouaction: On Sleeping[63]

The boys slept all day. Of course this was after a long trip, but it doesn't matter. Sleep is not something to feel guilty about doing. Sleep all you want. Sleep all day. Sleep all night. Sleep all weekend. It helps you stay up for days on end driving and drinking and smoking and loving and doing all the wonderful beat things there are to do in this world.

Suggested Kerouactivity:

Next time you're tired, sleep. Right then, no matter where you are or what you're doing (except while driving a car or operating heavy equipment, etc.). At work would be a fantastic place to catch a nap. Maybe you'll get fired, and then you can go go go *to your heart's content.*

---

63   There are other entries about sleep. Use the Table of Contents and find them yourself. I'm tired of all this cross-referencing.

DAY 64

Today's Kerouaction:
On Eating When Broke

When you're broke – which by the way is an excellent thing to experience once in your life – it doesn't mean you have to starve. Just the other day I walked in through the back door of a large donut chain and there sat large garbage cans full of (I assume) day-old donuts destined for the landfill. *Full!* So the ones in the middle had certainly not touched much of anything but other donuts. And even if they had, so what? It's good practice for your immune system. I've seen people garbage diving in pizza shops (e.g., in New Paltz, NY, where we hang out after climbing in The 'Gunks) and scoring excellent meals for free. You just have to get beyond your socially-constructed dignity and do what is necessary in order to eat. The survival instinct is strong. Use it.

Suggested Kerouactivity:

In the next 24 hours, retrieve some food out of a garbage can at home or a dumpster outside a restaurant and eat it. It's good practice for next time you are on the road.

DAY 65

Today's Kerouaction: On Books

You simply cannot have enough books. They are the one material possession that doesn't count as a material possession. That is, they don't count towards the earlier advice to be able to fit everything you own in your vehicle (see Day 10). And books are easily acquired these days. Libraries hold sales to clear room for the thousands of new books that assault them yearly. Sometimes you can buy a whole bag of books for a dollar (or some similarly cheap arrangement). And don't forget to take advantage of buying used books from yard sales or old bookstores or even on-line! Why buy anything new if you don't have to?[64] It's cheaper and better for the environment. And if you do acquire thousands of books, you can always give them away as gifts. When your place is full of books, and birthdays or other gift-giving holidays approach, just look around for a suitable gift, wrap it in anything but gift wrap (i.e., spare the environment and re-use something, like an old newspaper or a paper grocery bag), write the obligatory To and From and something unique directly on the paper (gift tags are for Martha Stewart wanna-be's), and honor the giftee with an original and meaningful present! A used Kerouac book, of course, would be best. A dog-eared, written-in tome of Edward Abbey's would do, also, as would a beat-up copy of *Fight Club*. Or anything from the References at the end of this book. Or this book!

---

64   Stealing is always an option, too (see Day 41).

Suggested Kerouactivity:

Start planning this very minute to give the gift of a book the next time you will be giving someone a present. Write down the name of the person, the occasion, and the title of the book below. Then get busy acquiring the book.

DAY 66

Today's Kerouaction: On Moving

Think about it: "...our one and only noble function of the time, *move*" (Kerouac, 1976a, p. 134). You've read the advice throughout this book to "*go go go!*"[65] This passage captures the essence of that advice. Keep moving. When in doubt, travel. Do not stop until you get there!

Have you visited Kerouac's birthplace, Lowell, Massachusetts? Have you visited the Jack Kerouac Commemorative in Kerouac Park, a part of Lowell National Historical Park? If not, *why not*? It is Mecca! *Mecca!*[66] The origin of beatness. Lightning in a bottle. Everything and nothing all at the same time and you could be there if you just simply . . . *move*.

Suggested Kerouactivity:

Figure out the location of the cemetery nearest where you are right now. Go there. Walk around. Read the headstones. Remember that some day you, too, will be reduced to a one-inch dash between dates. If you went to the cemetery, you moved. Now keep moving.

---

65   See Days 7, 19, 25, 32, 43, 47, 61, and 63.
66   If you've chosen to be offended by this reference, get over yourself. It's a colloquialism! A beat is anything *but* politically correct.

DAY 67

Today's Kerouaction: On Money for Gas

We've talked about hitchhiking as a means of travel, but this Kerouaction turns it into a strategy supporting travel in your own vehicle: pick up a hitchhiker and, in return, ask for gas money. Of course, in the United States these days a quarter would buy less than 1/16 of a gallon, which wouldn't get you very far. So, to account for inflation and the Bush administration's policies, expect a hitchhiker to kick in at least $4.00 (enough for about a gallon these days!) for a lift, maybe more depending on how far she wants to ride. It's beat to pick up a hitchhiker for kicks, too, as Neal and Dean and Mary Lou and Dunkel do. That's yet another passage in *On The Road* (1976a) for you to locate and read.

Suggested Kerouactivity:

Next time someone offers to give you gas money, ask them for a quarter. That might get an interesting conversation going. If it does, you might suggest they read this book!

DAY 68

Today's Kerouaction:
On Gasoline for Free

There's more than one way to score some gasoline for your road trip. One, of course, is to pick up hitchhikers in exchange for gas money (see Day 67). Another is to pump your tank full and drive off without paying.[67] Now that was probably a lot easier to get away with back in Kerouac's heyday, and certainly I am not recommending breaking the law or stealing. But it would be a very, very beat thing to do.

Suggested Kerouactivity:

Take a road trip. Do not fill up with gas first. Do not take any money or credit/debit cards. Just head out and keep going. Go go go until you run out of gas. Now figure out a way to get some gas. It will tap your beat ingenuity. An idea Crystal had was busking for money. That's where you perform some skill in public in return for money. You've seen musicians do it, playing on streetcorners with their instrument cases open. But you could read poetry, juggle, balance a chair on your nose, any number of things.

---

67   They call that a "drive-off" where I live, and they post signs saying that drive-offs will be prosecuted. See Footnote 2.

DAY 69

Today's Kerouaction: On Spontaneity

Can you picture a man carrying a woman around on piggyback, weaving in and out the tanks at a gas station while his comrades pump gas or go inside or wait in the car? I have never seen that! Maybe I have lived a sheltered life, but I am guessing that such spontaneous fun is a rarity in this over-compliant, stuffed-shirt, obsessive-compulsive, vain excuse for a society. Loosen up! Howl at the moon! Take a risk! Be spontaneous! Play piggyback with your sweetheart! Or like the anonymous saying advises, "Sing like no one is listening, dance like no one is watching, and love like you'll never get hurt." That's the beat way – live each moment like it's your last. What are you doing *right now* that honors life? Reading this book? You're not getting it, man!

Suggested Kerouactivity:

Go outside right now and skip down the sidewalk. Naked would be best. If anyone looks at you askance, tell them you're doing your Day 69 Kerouactivity. Of course, there's another way to honor Day 69, and I suspect you know what that might be without my spelling it out for you.

DAY 70

Today's Kerouaction: On the Ideal Bar

I cannot imagine a "dull" evening with Kerouac, let alone a "dull" bar in the French Quarter. But Old Bull sure didn't think an ideal bar existed in America at the time. The Kerouaction? Bar-hopping, of course. But not to the dullest bars you can find. Find the ones that fit Old Bull's description (Kerouac, 1976a, p. 147). Or the modern analogy.

What's that you ask? Well, it's not Applebee's, that's for sure. It's more likely a privately-owned, run down hole in the wall featuring ancient hardwood floors with nothing left of a stain except beer and dim lighting and a jukebox that only plays George Jones[68] and a clientele there for one reason: to drink and share a story. Such places exist in America today. They always will. Your job is to find one. Today. Have a beer for me.

Suggested Kerouactivity:

Become a regular at the nearest "ideal bar."[69] Drink the cheapest booze they have but tip the bartender well. <u>Always tip the bartender well</u>. It will pay off.

---

68   Another movie reference. Bet you can't solve this one. It's one of my *favorite* movies. Lots of beat characters.
69   I'm a regular at two: The Depot and Mark's Brother's. They are 600 miles apart, so I don't want to hear excuses about distance.

DAY 71

Today's Kerouaction: On Recycling

Old Bull Lee uses a hammer on a huge piece of thick rotten wood to remove nails, "millions of them," in order to build a shelf that won't collapse in six months under the weight of knickknacks. He opines about the shoddy quality of goods – even though "they could make houses that last *forever*" (Kerouac, 1976a, p. 149). So what has changed since the 1950s?

Not a blessed thing. Everyone knows about "planned obsolescence," yet most people keep right on buying "new stuff": cars, stereos, and gadgets (white kitchen machinery) that end up in the landfill. Or worse, littering the side of a once-pristine hill in the woods. We have such an eyesore a minute's walk from my former house in Pennsylvania, along a beautiful lazy river and a Hike and Bike Trail built by the Army Corps of Engineers. As you walk the trail past the backyards of adjoining private properties, you can see where the homeowners turned a hill in their woods into their own cemetery for "stuff": old bathtubs, windows, appliances, and whatever else they no longer needed and either couldn't sell or give away[70] or couldn't be bothered to try.

The Kerouaction implied here is this: recycle and reuse! You can live more cheaply that way – definitely a beat thing to do – and

---

70   At the last two places I lived – Mansfield, PA and Gardiner, ME – all I had to do was put "stuff" out in front of my house with a sign reading "FREE" and it magically disappeared. One time I put out an old TV cart with wheels and some young men rode it down the street, crashed it, and left it there. That didn't meet my needs, but it sure was a beat thing to do.

you help preserve the environment for future beat generations at the same time. Shop at the Salvation Army for clothes, use comic pages for wrapping paper, put your glass and plastic and metal out for recycling, give away your old stuff whenever possible instead of sending it to the landfill, find your next backpack at a thrift store, and just generally *simplify* your life of material goods so you can fit everything you own in your car (see Day 10).

Suggested Kerouactivity:

Make a list of all the things you've recycled this week. If the list is short, you know what to do to make it longer. If it's long, you're already beat (but you could always be beater).

DAY 72

Today's Kerouaction: On Cats

Kerouac loved cats. (Old Bull loved cats, too, but not always for the best reasons.) Indeed, Jack's angst at the death of his pet cat, Tyke, was the subject of several pages in *Big Sur* (1992).

There is a famous picture of Kerouac wearing his trademark flannel shirt and holding a cat. It adorns the cover of a book titled, *The Kerouac We Knew* (1987). Cats are cool![71] They epitomize beatness in domesticated pets because they follow their own path. Eckhart Tolle claims that cats are zen masters (see Day 14). Have at least two cats in the house (so they can keep each other company when you are "on the road"). Name one Kerouac and name the other Dharma. Or some other Kerouacian name or phrase.[72]

Suggested Kerouactivity:

If you already have a cat, go pet him or her right now. If you don't, go to your nearest animal shelter and get one or two. You already know what to name them.

---

71   By the way – and this is going to piss off some of my friends – if a person doesn't like cats, they are not beat. Period. In fact, I distrust anyone who claims to hate cats. They are either lying or they have some deep psychological trauma preventing them from seeing the truth: cats are cool. And no, that is not a reference to a song by the band Squeeze.
72   My current cats' names are Karma and Emma. Can you guess which one I named?

DAY 73

Today's Kerouaction:
On Visions and Playing the Horses

Trust your hunches! Trust your gut! Follow your gut! Follow your intuition! Follow your heart!

Those are the general Kerouactions we can discern from a horse-racing passage in *On The Road* (1976a). More specifically, bet horses by name. That is, pick a name from the line-up that jumps out at you because it reminds you of something or someone important or significant in your life (probably relating to Jung's concept of "synchronicity"). Hey, that's got to work as well as any other system (since after all it *is* called "gambling"). An ex-wife of mine had a grandmother who always bet on the grey horse in a race. Or, on one that shit prior to the race (less weight to carry around the track?).

What does your gut tell you to do *right now*? Go do it.

Suggested Kerouactivity:

Go to a racetrack. Get a racing form and scan the horses' names. Bet on one whose name jumps out at you. Bet to win (not place or show). Send me half your winnings.

DAY 74

Today's Kerouaction: On Games

Even in our over-amped, video game-ridden, ultra-competitive culture, all it really takes to have fun is will and imagination. Look around you for opportunities. Put a tennis ball (or anything similar) in the toe of an old sock and launch it back-and-forth by holding on to the other end. If you can throw it or climb it or jump over it, you have the making of a game or a contest. I rather think the beats would have appreciated footbag[73] if it had been invented at the time (it didn't come along until 1972). A footbag or a beanbag can provide hours of fun, exercise, and good times socializing.

Suggested Kerouactivity:

Invent a beat game and describe it below. Stay thin on "rules." Rules are for squares.

---

73   Yes, footbag. Not Hacky Sack. The latter is a trade name, not a generic one. Not all footbags are Hacky Sacks (and not all facial tissues are Kleenex and not all copying is Xeroxing). By the way, SandMaster is the best footbag.

DAY 75

Today's Kerouaction: On Trip Necessities

Far be it from me to suggest stealing out of necessity, but of course that would certainly be a beat thing to do. Rather, the "legal" discernable Kerouaction is that little is needed for a trip cross country: gas and oil for the car, bread and cheese for the body, and cigarettes for the psyche. Beyond that, good company is in order if you can swing it. So gas up the clunker, stock up with a loaf of bread and a jar of Cheez Whiz, grab a carton of cigarettes and take off for the other coast. Nothing but those things, please. No suitcase full of clothes. No toiletries. No map. No cell phone. Just food, gas, cigarettes. See what you can do without! *That* is a beat thing to do. And it's probably illegal as Hell, too, if you don't carry I.D.[74] and enough money to keep you from being labeled a "vagrant." The main thing is spontaneity and passion: decide and then *go go go*.

Suggested Kerouactivity:

Even if you are not going to take off right away, buy yourself a jar of Cheez Whiz and store it away for that day when you finally heed the advice contained herein. Then all you need to do is buy bread and cigarettes, gas up and go go go.[75]

---

74   Especially ID approved by "Homeland Security." What country do we live in? I need a reminder.

75   FYI, unopened Cheez Whiz will stay good way beyond your lifespan, so no worries about it going bad if you procrastinate heading out on the road.

DAY 76

Today's Kerouaction: On Nudity

When is the last time you ran around outside naked yipping and leaping and digging this old world? What? You've never done that? Or at least not since you were two years old? Well, today, run around outside naked. If you're worried about getting arrested (which would actually be a very beat thing to do), find a secluded spot. Run around in your birthday suit. Yell a lot. Experience freedom. One of my friends likes to go into pizza joints naked and order a pie. He gets a lot of weird looks when he does that. The last time I'm aware he did it was in Albany, NY, in 2005. And they served him! I don't know how he does stuff like that without getting arrested, but it's certainly a Kerouaction and one that Jack would approve!

Suggested Kerouactivity:

Get comfortable with nudity. Visit a nude beach or a strip club and notice your thoughts (but don't judge them!).

DAY 77

Today's Kerouaction: On Travel Rest

Who needs money for motels or a tent or a sleeping bag or a camper or RV or Winnebago or VW Westfalia? When you are on the road, and you run out of steam, park the car and sleep until you wake up. Then get moving again. It's that simple. You save time setting up camp or checking into a motel, you save money on campground and lodging fees, and you get to pick the view you wish to see when you wake up. It's the beat way to travel.

Suggested Kerouactivity:

Start keeping a pillow and a sleeping bag (or a blanket) in your vehicle at all times. You never know when you might decide to <u>go go go</u> and rest may become a necessity.

DAY 78

Today's Kerouaction:
On Gas Money and Birthday Presents

A true present is to be used by the recipient as she or he sees fit. So when you need gas money on the road, pawn something, even if it was a "birthday present." And pay attention to synchronicity. When you need something and a way to meet that need presents itself out of the blue, don't second guess it: take advantage.

Suggested Kerouactivity:

Find out where your nearest pawn shop is and pay a visit. Sell something. Buy something with the proceeds. This will be good practice for the day when it might become necessary for survival.

DAY 79

Today's Kerouaction: On Energy Conservation

With gasoline prices over $4 per gallon as I write this, I find it heartening that one is almost forced to be green when living beat. Energy costs money, and when you are living on a shoestring (or less!), every bit of energy conservation translates to cost savings.

So turn off that engine and coast downhill. You'll save money and maybe you'll scare yourself while you're at it. Scare yourself at least once a day. (I'm not sure that's a beat thing to do but it's a good motto nonetheless, one I credit my friend Keith for making me aware of and that I have seen attributed to Eleanor Roosevelt but I've come to doubt she was the originator.)

Suggested Kerouactivity:

Scare yourself before going to bed tonight. Think of something you fear doing, and do it. Say hi to a stranger. Sing in public. Call your ex-spouse. Invest in the stock market. Run around your house naked. Dress funny and go to the store. It doesn't matter what you do, as long as it scares you to do it.

DAY 80

Today's Kerouaction: On Improvisation

We've already discussed the "beat diet," but on occasion it's desirable to have hot food and a passage in *On The Road* (1976a) demonstrates the importance of improvisation. Heat is heat. You can heat a can of food in any number of ways. A hot iron is one of them, but why couldn't you put a can on the engine block of your car?[76] And speaking of campfires, since you are likely going to be outside whenever possible, a campfire is another possibility. But there are others - look around you and see. Improvisation like this is at the heart of "traveling light," an essential Kerouaction on the path to beatness.

Suggested Kerouactivity:

Take up the habit of doing without new "stuff" by making do with the old. My mother's words echo: "Use it up, wear it out, make it do or do without." Learn to improvise instead of wasting gas driving to Wal-Mart and accumulating more stuff that will end up in the landfill.

---

76   Don't forget to put some holes in the can or you will have an event under the hood that mirrors one of Edward Abbey's stories about pork and beans heated in a campfire and beans dripping from the trees.

DAY 81

Today's Kerouaction: On Making Do

Starving, no money, no smokes. I met a guy the other day in Gardiner, ME who said he had been around the country a few times back in the 60s by going as far as he could on what little money he had and then staying there until he found a way to go farther. The going isn't so tough – there is always your thumb. Water? Find a stream. Food? Beg, borrow, or steal it. Tobacco? Same as food, and in this case, the Kerouaction is not only thrifty but "green" as well: you're helping clean up the environment when you find butts on the ground and smoke them!

Suggested Kerouactivity:

Today, smoke a butt you find on the ground or eat some food you find in the garbage in preparation for the next time you are on the road.

DAY 82

Today's Kerouaction: On Greeting the Morning

Beats don't fear nakedness. There is a sacredness to nakedness (unintended rhyme there but I will leave it). What better way to greet a morning or say farewell to a sunset or pay tribute to a soaring monolith than "skyclad" (my favorite Wiccan word). Take your clothes off. Right now. No matter where you are or what you are doing. If someone says anything to you about it, or so much as casts a dirty or inquisitive look your way, tell them the book you are reading just told you to do it. Then tell them where they can buy it. Or give them your copy and buy another one. Unless you want to steal one, which indeed would be a very beat thing to do.

Suggested Kerouactivity:

Next sunrise, stand in the window (or outside!) naked and enjoy the warm rays on your skin. You might like it so much that you take to doing it every day. For a real unique sunrise, come to Maine. We get the first one every day (in the U.S.).

DAY 83

Today's Kerouaction: On Time

"What time is it?" I ask. "Now," replies my great friend, Keith, the inspiration for this book. It is his way of reminding me what we both know: that time is a delusion and a real beat does not allow the clock to dictate behavior. It is always now. So what is it you want to do this very moment? Is it 8 A.M. and you want a beer? Drink up! Is it 2 A.M. and you want to talk to your friend who is likely sound asleep? Call! Is it the middle of the work day and you are tired? Sleep! Is it dinnertime and you are hungry for pancakes and eggs? Get the frying pan heated up and get cooking!

Do not put off doing something because of what time it is on a clock. *Now* is the best – and the only – time you can do anything. Like the song says, "It's five o'clock somewhere." Live in the moment.

Suggested Kerouactivity:

What would you do <u>right now</u> except that it's the "wrong" time of day? Can't think of anything? Think harder. There's got to be something. Once you figure out what it is, do it.

DAY 84

Today's Kerouaction:
On Unconditional Love

Find someone to love and be loved by *unconditionally*. Someone who understands that no one else is responsible for your feelings. No one causes you to be happy, sad, angry, bitter, etc. You do that to yourself with the delusional stories your mind is weaving. Find someone that lets you be yourself. And do the same for him or her. If they do things you don't like, don't mistake that for them. It's a behavior. Not the beautiful being you love. If they are happy, be happy they are happy, even if they come home in the middle of the night drunk with a bunch of strangers and want to stay up all night talking. So what? It just is what it is. Resisting it is what causes suffering. And relationship breakdowns!

Suggested Kerouactivity:

Research what Carl Rogers said about sunsets and people. Research what Krishnamurti said about measuring love and thereby destroying it. Write down what they said below. There is a way beyond what you've been taught where relationships are concerned. It's been written down. And you can read it and live it.

DAY 85

Today's Kerouaction: On IT

Dean and Sal are sitting in the back of a travel bureau car at the beginning of their way back East. Dean has been going on about IT. What is IT? I can't explain it with concepts and even if I could you couldn't understand it with your mind. Maybe it's that state where you find yourself and you lose yourself, like Bodhi talks about in the movie, *Point Break*.[77] Or maybe it's the state Mihaly Csikszentmihalyi calls "flow" (1991). Or maybe it's the state of no mind, beginner's mind, where you know everything and you know nothing and you know that this moment is everything and nothing at the same time and words don't matter at all. It is understanding without words,[78] without thought, like when you and a friend both experience something and look at each other and words are unnecessary.

But what's the Kerouaction, you ask? Be fully present every moment. Experience everything like you were going to die tomorrow. See, feel, smell, hear, and taste with reckless abandon whatever is in this moment. Things are fine just like they are, right this minute, right *now*. And there is no need to label what *is*. As Alan Watts pointed out, the sound of the rain needs no explanation.

Suggested Kerouactivity:

If I gave you an assignment for this entry, it would mean I don't get IT. Get IT?

---

77   An excellent "beat" movie.
78   See especially the work of J. Krishnamurti.

DAY 86

Today's Kerouaction: On "The Road"

"The Road" is symbolic of action. Of mindful travel (see Day 85 regarding IT) with no other purpose than experiencing each moment as you *go go go*.

Today's Kerouaction: *go go go*. No plan. No suitcase. No map. No itinerary. Just head out and see where you end up. In my youth I was enamored of a TV drama series titled *Then Came Bronson*, starring a young Michael Parks. He epitomized something for me at the time that I later realized was the essence of living in the moment and traveling as suggested here. At the beginning of each episode, Bronson is stopped at a red light and a sedan pulls alongside. Inside is a businessman, who asks him where he is headed, to which Bronson replies, "Wherever I end up, I guess."

"Wish I were you," replies the businessman.

Don't wish you were Bronson. Or Dean. Or Sal. *Be* them. Start now.

Suggested Kerouactivity:

Watch an episode of <u>Then Came Bronson</u>. *See if it inspires you to* <u>go go go</u>.

DAY 87

Today's Kerouaction:
On Kidney Function

Even in seemingly insignificant passages of *On The Road* lurk potential beat actions. For one thing, seek out restaurants with bathrooms the size of a ship's galley (there's one in Camden, ME). This will likely correlate to the prices on the menu: the bigger the bathroom, the pricier the food. The latter consideration is, of course, extremely important when you are on the road without a dime in your pocket. For another thing, it is easy to find entertainment in the simplest situations (or, in this case, from the most basic bodily functions).

Now in this case Dean advises that stopping yourself midstream in order to change urinals is damaging to the kidneys. Which, of course, given the importance of alcohol in the beat lifestyle – and the attendant need for kidney function – is something to consider. Or not. Something's going to kill you, and some would suggest that this "trick" accomplishes the same thing as Kegel exercises, noted to enhance sexual performance and pleasure. Jack would dig that.

Suggested Kerouactivity:

Next time you are in a bathroom with multiple input devices, see how many you can "christen" (and without any spillage!).

DAY 88

Today's Kerouaction: On Dress

The place: a carnival in Denver on Alameda Boulevard at Federal. Now, I have never been to Denver, but when I visit there some day you can bet I will throw on tight Levis and a T-shirt and go find the exact spot where Sal and Dean dug the merry-go-rounds and Ferris wheels and popcorn and other carnival sights and sounds. In the meantime, it's jeans and T-shirts for me, and I hope for you as well because you can't get much beater than that regarding dress.

Suggested Kerouactivity:

Go through your clothing and separate the jeans and T-shirts from the rest. Donate everything else to Goodwill or the Salvation Army. Oh, and keep any red plaid wool shirts you find, too.

DAY 89

Today's Kerouaction: On Sleep

A student asked his master, "What is enlightenment?"

The master replied, "When hungry, eat. When tired, sleep."

This classic zen saying captures the Kerouaction in this passage with the fewest words possible. When you're tired, sleep right then and where you are. What else is there to say?

Suggested Kerouactivity:

Count how many times Kerouac mentions sleeping in On The Road *(1976a).*

DAY 90

Today's Kerouaction:
On Cheap Travel

The boys traveled using "travel bureau" cars. Travel bureaus were agencies that connected cars that needed to move from one place to another with people with the same need. That is, if you needed to get from L.A. to New York, you contacted the travel bureau to see if someone had a car they needed driven from L.A. to New York.

Such services still exist! So if you want to *go go go*, and you have a driver's license, and you're not too fussy about where you go or when, you can be "on the road" with minimal transportation expenses – even in 2008.

It's up to you whether you want to christen your wheels with a fling in broad daylight like Dean; but, of course, that would be the beatest thing to do.

Suggested Kerouactivity:

Get on-line and check out companies that put drivers together with people who need their cars moved. Don't have a computer? Good. Go to the library and use theirs.

DAY 91

Today's Kerouaction:
On Picking Up Hitchhikers

Since it's beat to hitchhike (see Day 25), it's beat to pick up hitchhikers, too. Make them pay for gas, though. With today's gas prices, feel free to require more than 4 bits.

Suggested Kerouactivity:

Pick up the next hitchhiker you see. Tell them this book told you to do it. And if the hitchhiker tells you an interesting story, document it below (see Day 25).

DAY 92

Today's Kerouaction: On Appearances

Sometimes multiple Kerouactions can be discerned from short passages. Regarding appearances:

1. Stop shaving so often.
2. Go around barechested, especially while driving (Microsoft Word tried to hyphenate that word, but, as a small Kerouaction, I am leaving it as Jack wrote it).
3. Hang out with bums.

Suggested Kerouactivity:

Pick one of the above and act on it today. Resolve to accomplish all three by week's end. Can't find a bum? Be *the bum.*[79]

---

79   A veiled movie reference. Good luck on this one.

DAY 93

Today's Kerouaction: On Driving

Pick two points and see if you can average 70 miles per hour between them. Obviously – if you're following along – Denver to Chicago is the preferred route, but feel free to choose two points closer to where you live. Or, as a compromise, pick any two locations from Jack's travels. Harrisburg, PA, to Washington, DC, maybe? I'd love to see someone average 70 on *that* trip! It would be a very beat thing to do. But don't ask me to bail you out of jail!

Suggested Kerouactivity:

Next time you are driving, clock the time it takes you to go from point A to point B. Divide the time it took you into the distance to figure out your average speed. If your average speed was above the speed limit, you drove beat. If you're a rider and not a driver, you can still do the computation and prevail on the driver to try to average over the speed limit. Note: if you're driving in Los Angeles, forget this assignment. No one can average over the speed limit in L.A.!

DAY 94

Today's Kerouaction: On Parking

If you have a car – which is a big if – and you find it useful to park it (remember, better to be on the move), park it with the front end pointed in the direction you intend to go. That is, park your car ready to *go go go*.

Now as I'm sure you're aware, some parking areas have rules posted that say you may not back into parking spaces. If you've been with me this far, I don't need to go into the Kerouaction regarding compliance with that particular rule.

However, why park in a "dark spot" (Kerouac, 1976a, p. 237)? In the referenced case, it was probably to conceal the car since where it was parked was likely not a "societally-approved location" (p. 237). But it's certainly not a bad idea to park in the shade for pragmatic reasons, especially in the summer months. Hot upholstery sucks.

Suggested Kerouactivity:

Next time you have to park your car, park it pointed in the direction you're headed and in a dark spot. If you get a ticket, do what you think Jack would do.

DAY 95

Today's Kerouaction:
On Listening to Music

Listening to musicians, Dean tells them to "go, go, go" (Kerouac, 1976a, p. 241).

Throughout this book you've seen the advice to *go go go*.[80] Now you know the genesis of that phrase. But more importantly, this book would not be complete without an entry about music.

The boys listened to music a lot. Mostly jazz. So listening to music is a beat thing to do, especially jazz. Seek out a dark, seedy barroom and listen to the old stuff.

Suggested Kerouactivity:

Find a way to listen to Charlie Parker and do it. Today. I bet your library has some. Or listen on-line (the library's good for that, too).

---

80   See Days 7, 19, 25, 32, 43, 47, 61, 63, 66, 68, 75, 77, 86, 90, and 94.

DAY 96

Today's Kerouaction:
On Sleeping Arrangements

When you need a place to crash – inside, that is – a movie theatre will provide shelter (and relative darkness) in a pinch. Now I'm not sure you'll find all-night movies in too many places, and certainly not for admission under half-a-buck, but the concept is still relevant. Contrast paying $7.50 for movie theatre admission (yes, you can still get away with staying for multiple showings) with the cost of a motel room!

Suggested Kerouactivity:

Go to a movie you don't care about and practice sleeping in the theater. Sneak in if you don't have cash.

DAY 97

Today's Kerouaction:
On "Digging the Ride"

"Dig the ride" (Kerouac, 1976a, p. 284). This is not so much something you actively "do" as it is a way of being. That is – and this is certainly a zen-like approach – in every situation, there is a way to accept *what is*. Even enjoy it. Whereas the car the boys were driving through Mexico bounced and swayed like a ship in choppy seas, there was no point in resisting the matter. Why not just go with the flow?

Now, at this point the boys were pretty stoned, and that certainly makes it easier to take a mellow view of things. But mind-altering drugs are not essential. You can accept what is right now without the aid of a guru, drugs, god, or a meditation system.[81] Dig the ride.

Suggested Kerouactivity:

Enter into a contract with a staircase and practice digging the ride. Thich Nhat Hanh talks of this in one of his dharma talks:

> In Plum Village many of us begin by signing a contract with a staircase: that is, you make a vow that you will always go up or down that staircase very mindfully, with very solid steps. If it happens that halfway up you realize that one of your steps has not been very solid, you will go down, and

---

81   Again, see J. Krishnamurti's work. Please.

begin again. And if you succeed in that, then wherever you go you will be able to dwell in the present moment.[82]

---

82   According to my Internet source, this is from his August 6, 1998 Dharma Talk.

DAY 98

Today's Kerouaction: On Hygiene

So you're on the road and sleeping in the car or out under the stars (forsaking motels and the like) and you need a shower. Maybe you just spent the night at a whorehouse like the boys did right before stopping at a bathhouse. While hygiene is not a priority on the road, occasionally it feels pretty good to wash off the road dust (or other substances). America still has lots of places where you can grab a shower. In the summer, campgrounds and public swimming pools are options. Yes, there's an entry fee. Maybe you can sneak in. Or charm the person at the gate.

On the other hand, why not just jump in the nearest stream, river, lake, or ocean. Take a bar of biodegradable soap in with you and wash to your heart's content.

Suggested Kerouactivity:

Right now, put a bar of Tom's of Maine soap in your rucksack so next time you head out you'll be hygienically prepared.

DAY 99

Today's Kerouaction: On Barter[83]

Never forget the maxim about one man's trash being another man's treasure. When you see something you want, why jump to purchase it? Think about what you have that might be of value to the owner of that something, and suggest a trade. Where tangible goods are concerned, it's a green thing to do (see Days 18, 79, and 81) since it doesn't rely on the creation of new material things. It's recycling! But don't forget you can barter services, too. Do you know how to do something and need something done? Barter a service. How about writing someone a poem in return for a haircut? Or shoveling someone's sidewalk for a good meal?

The beats were green before green was cool.

Suggested Kerouactivity:

Make a list in this space of all the things you could barter with (material goods and services). Next time you need something from someone else, check back on this page and see if you have something you can barter for it.

---

83   See also Day 59.

DAY 100

Today's Kerouaction: On Uncertainty

If you're reading this, you're alive. If you're reading this, there's one thing you can be certain about: you'll die. Other than that, there is no certainty. Can you be secure in that? Knowing that there is no security? Knowing that everything is happening to everyone at the same time right now in this big world and it can't be any different from how it is?

Suggested Kerouactivity:

As I take my leave of your kind consideration, please think about revisiting these pages on occasion. They might take on a different meaning for you from time to time. Perhaps a seed has been planted and will take root and when you run into the plant some day you'll say something like "the only people for me are the mad ones . . ." (Kerouac, 1976a, p. 8).

REFERENCES

Blanton, B. (1996). *Radical honesty: How to transform your life by telling the truth*. New York: Dell Publishing.

Csikszentmihalyi, M. (1991). *Flow: The psychology of optimal experience*. New York: Harper

Hanh, T.N. (1996). *The long road turns to joy: A guide to walking meditation*. Berkeley, CA: Parallax Press.

Kerouac, J. (1992). *Big Sur*. New York: Penguin Books.

Kerouac, J. (1976). *On the road*. New York: Penguin Books.

Kerouac, J. (1976). *The dharma bums*. New York: Penguin Books.

Krishnamurti, J. (1973). *Beyond violence*. India: Krishnamurti Foundation.

Krishnamurti, J. (2000). *To be human*. Boston: Shambhala.

London, J. (1903). *The call of the wild*. New York: Grosset & Dunlap.

McCleary, J.B. (2002). *The hippie dictionary*. Berkeley, CA: Ten Speed Press.

Meyer, K. (1994). *How to take a shit in the woods: An environmentally sound approach to a lost art*. Berkeley, CA: Ten Speed Press.

Montgomery, J. (1987). *The Kerouac we knew*. San Anselmo, CA: Fels & Firn Press.

Nicosia, G. (1994). *Memory babe: A critical biography of Jack Kerouac*. Los Angeles: University of California Press.

Rosenberg, M. (2005). *Nonviolent communication: A language of life*. Encinitas, CA: PuddleDancer Press.

Tolle, E. (1999). *The power of now: A guide to spiritual enlightenment*. Novato, CA: New World Library.

Washburn, J. (2005). *University, Inc.: The corporate corruption of higher education*. Cambridge, MA: Basic Books.

Watts, A. (2000). *An introduction to meditation*. Novato, CA: New World Library.

Williamson, M. (1996). *A return to love: Reflection on the principles of "A Course in Miracles."* Perennial Currents.

ABOUT THE AUTHOR

Rick Dale has a D.Ed. in Educational Administration from Pennsylvania State University, and is a professor in the Special Education Department at a state university in Maine. He is a Jack Kerouac enthusiast who plays bluegrass music semi-professionally and enjoys a multitude of outdoor sports. Rick lives with his partner and her two sons—and two cats—on a lake in Maine. This is his first book.

Made in the USA